THE SCOPE STATEMENT

THE
SCOPE
STATEMENT

How to Renovate Your Home
without Breaking Your Budget

DAMIAN CARROLL

THE SCOPE STATEMENT

How to Renovate Your Home without Breaking Your Budget

ISBN   978-1-5445-2249-4 *Paperback*
       978-1-5445-2248-7 *Ebook*

For Steve, who is no longer around to see the results of this book and his training. I hope you'd be proud of how things have turned out!

CONTENTS

INTRODUCTION

There are millions of home improvement projects undertaken across the world every year. It is a multibillion-dollar industry (probably trillions, really) that has spawned over time, and you can see dozens of TV shows on any channel anywhere in the world.

However, one thing I've noticed in having a career in the construction industry for many years—there appears to be no real noticeable improvement in the bad experiences people have.

For example:

"I don't understand why the budget has blown out."

"I'm not sure why I've been sent a variation/change order from the contractor for moving an old pipe."

"Why is the municipality making me upgrade my sewer lateral? And what does that even mean?"

These concerns only scratch the surface, and each one seems rather painful.

Most of these items and the issues that occur when doing a home upgrade are usually due to a lack of research and understanding. It's not the rookie's fault.

For those who are new to doing home upgrades, the road ahead can seem mind boggling.

- What do I want?
- Where do I find the information I need?
- What do I do with it once I've found it?
- How does it all fit together?

The confusion can be endless.

Even if you do figure this out, another source of frustration that occurs is the sizable gap in expectations—from the owner(s) of what they *want* done compared to the realities of the builder/general contractor in terms of what *needs* to be done. This causes significant budget overruns and a general sour taste in the owner's mouth when the budget is blown to smithereens!

My aim is to reduce the expectation gap as much as possible by providing a focused approach for those who are preparing to do a home renovation of any kind. It's what's known in the industry as a scope statement.

A scope statement is a document that clearly lays out all the deliverables that are needed for a project to be completed. It also ties the related tasks together.

For example: demolishing your kitchen? Before you start, you need to make sure the plumbing fixtures have been made safe or turned off and isolated. Otherwise, there will be oceans of water in your house when the demolition work starts! Essentially, the plumber needs to show up before any demolition work begins. Your providers (builders, consultants, subtrades, etc.) should know that. Still, you need to make absolutely sure there is no ambiguity. Same with the electrician for all things power.

Three key items you should obtain when writing a scope statement:

- As the client, you need to tell the world what you want.
- The providers know what they are to supply and install.
- Acquire reliable pricing before you start—fewer surprises later.

Here are several questions for you to ask before reading this book:

- Will this book cover all issues?
- Will this methodology be for everyone?
- Will it work every time?
- Am I telling you this is the holy grail and the ultimate problem solver?

An emphatic no to all of the above.

However, are you going to learn a lot reading this book? I'd like to think so!

One thing I'm absolutely certain of is that I've lost count of the number of times writing a scope statement has gotten me out of trouble.

I've seen many "scopes" for projects issued via bullet-point emails. Unfortunately, this is lazy and simply doesn't cut it. There is too much ambiguity that sits behind a "task." For example, a task on an email might read, "A new bathtub." Great and wonderfully descriptive, isn't it? Alas, that doesn't tell anyone anything.

Here are the types of things this task needs to flesh out:

- Is there a bathtub currently installed?

- If so, how big is it?
- How big do you want the new one?
- Where do you want it?
- Where are the existing water lines, waste line, and vent?

I've just asked five questions from that one "task." The builder can't proceed until they know this information. Otherwise, they're guessing. Deciding you want a new bathtub is just one small part of the process.

The point here is that if you're unprepared, the entire job will look confusing and cost more time and money. No one wants that.

You are going to make mistakes, for sure, but don't stress about it. Treat it as a learning curve for doing the next one. My key intent for this book is to help you understand the importance of capturing as much information as possible about the job up front before you start.

But be warned fairly and squarely: there will be effort required by you. I won't sugarcoat this by saying there's a magic wand you can buy on Amazon or at 7-Eleven that can do it for you. It's like everything in life: the more you put in, the more you get out.

This is not meant to scare you. I've provided a real-life example later in the book to help ease the confusion and pain of not knowing what it's all about. I plan to provide you with the aha moment.

There will be pain, no doubt about it. There is no construction job anywhere without some anguish. However, I'm confident this book will reduce it somewhat and make your home upgrade a much more enjoyable experience and maybe even a bit of fun.

Some may read this and say it's rubbish. That's fine with me. I'm under no illusions that I know it all.

However, I know that in all facets of life, the 7 Ps apply: Proper Planning and Preparation Prevents Piss-Poor Performance.

I'd have the 7 Ps in the front of your mind when next contemplating an upgrade to your home for a new bathroom, kitchen, etc.

CHAPTER ONE

MY BACKGROUND

So why would anyone listen to me? Fair question.

I have a marketing degree, diploma in accounting, diploma in project management, hold a builder's license in Australia, and I'm also a member of the CIOB (Chartered Institute of Builders). So I'd like to think there is some substance to what I can offer.

Importantly, I've been working in the construction industry in one way, shape, or form for the past fifteen-plus years. This has been in both Australia (my native country) and the USA (my adopted country).

How did I get there? I dabbled in construction work of fluctuating degrees over a number of years but had not focused on it. I knew I liked the concept of project management because of the varied work one gets—the same monotonous daily tasks just aren't for me.

I was, at a point in time, in between jobs and at a critical juncture financially with the fuel tank warning light flashing red. On my knees, ready for the knockout blow, I was fortunate enough to come across a gentleman who gave me a chance for a formal "education" in the construction industry.

He ended up being my mentor, and I still regard him the most influential teacher about construction I've ever had. He has forgotten more than I, and most other people in the industry, will ever know.

Unfortunately, he was struck down with cancer and did not make it to see this book written. I hope he would have approved.

So what did he do? He taught me the PMBOK system and how to apply it in the construction industry. The term means Project Management Body of Knowledge.

PMBOK has nine functions. You can use it to purchase a newspaper or construct a one-hundred-story building. I didn't believe it regarding the newspaper, so he tested me on this one day. We went through each function of buying the newspaper, and sure enough, it was applicable. Who knew…Anyway, that was an expensive and humbling lunch that cost me, but it was well worth it.

As well as working on the commercial side of the construction game, I've owned a number of properties over the years and have undertaken several different projects, from landscaping to kitchen upgrades to bathroom remodels. So I've had a crack at a few things. Have I gotten it right every time? No. Have I learned something each time? You bet.

The beauty of this industry is that you learn something new each and every day. There are many, many wonderful people who can't do enough to help you by passing on their experience and knowledge. The key is being able to find these folks and listen to what they have to say. I've been fortunate that wherever I've gone, many people have been willing to help and teach me along the way.

I'm hoping to pass on something of what I've learned to those who need the help. It's not what I know. It's what others have taught me. That is the key point out of all this.

CHAPTER TWO

THE NEED FOR PREPLANNING

It doesn't matter how much you think you do or don't know. Your project(s) will be a disaster without the proper planning in place.

THE TWO MOST IMPORTANT AREAS OF ANY PROJECT

1. The scope (what are you doing)

2. The cost (how much)

I recently prepared detailed scope statements and financial budgets for commercial clients that entailed various building and property upgrades. These included essential building infrastructures (boilers, cooling towers, etc.) as well as water-proofing under existing exterior facades, among other things.

The scope statement provided clarity for the respective clients about the enormity of the tasks and their intricate nature. This allowed corresponding trades to provide fair and reasonable costs, with the aim of keeping variations/change orders to a minimum. It allowed us to set a sensible budget for the project that was realistic, fair, and told the true story.

So what does all this mean? If you want your project to be as successful as possible, you will have to put in some work up front. There is no getting around that. Period! I am going to repeat myself on this point throughout the book. It is deliberate, and I will not apologize.

Years of experience have taught me that this needs to happen—no exceptions. Set aside the time and do it. It's not as daunting as it seems. Like writing this book, once I started, it actually wasn't that bad. It ended up being fun. I learned plenty and met some wonderful people along the way. The same can happen to you with your home project.

You will have no end of pain if you think that you can undertake a project of any size, such as a bathroom, kitchen, and so forth, and complete the upgrade without any planning. I guarantee it.

The more time you put into your project up front, the more you will understand it, and the more you will save yourself the pain of your expectation (low cost) versus the reality of actually doing it (higher cost).

Having written hundreds and hundreds of scope statements, experience has shown me the value of spending the time doing this. In short, the client understood what they were buying, and the supplier(s) knew what they were expected to provide.

What does compiling a scope statement and budget estimate mean for you? What does it look like?

Get your mind into the position that preparing a scope statement will probably take the equivalent of two to three days in total (sixteen to twenty-four hours). Might be more, might be less. Understand that those time requirements do not occur all at once but in total.

It doesn't matter if it's done over the course of any number of weeks or months. Whatever makes you feel comfortable. My advice is, don't worry about the time commitment because you can go as fast or as slow as you want. But do the work.

The scope needs to be completed first, and then you can work out the cost associated with each task. The budget estimate might take a similar amount of time as the scope (sixteen to twenty-four hours) to assemble all the data you need. Once again, take your time on this and don't cut corners.

The detail provided in the ensuing pages will help you navigate how to find the information you need. The respective examples will show you how it's compiled into a cohesive document.

It's all there for you, so let's get going.

CHAPTER THREE

THE SCOPE STATEMENT

This is the meat of the project and the purpose of the book. The success to putting together a scope statement is to look at each component of a finished product and then peel back the layers that make it up.

The included example is one for a bathroom. It is real as this was my own bathroom at home. It considers the respective subtrades that are required to do the work and then what each of them needs to do and how it all ties together.

Okay, so where do you begin and how do you put one together?

The best thing to start with is having the end in mind. Some good questions to ask to get this process going are:

- What do you want to achieve?
- How do you want the finished product to look?
- What functionality do you want it to serve?
- Who is going to use it?
- Do you want it to be a feature of the house?

A wonderful place to start to get answers to these questions is by accessing Houzz (www.houzz.com). They have lots of ideas and will assist you immensely in answering the what.

On their website, go to the search bar and type in "bathroom model ideas." Start looking through the examples shown. It will get you thinking about what you want.

Note that the research can take as long as you like. It can be quite fun looking at all the options available, so try not to view it as a chore. There are lots of other internet websites that can help you as well if you don't like Houzz. You are limited only by your own imagination.

Once you've figured out the basic look of the bathroom you want, you're now ready to start putting this together.

If you've never done a remodel of any type, it's going to be hard to know what you're looking at. No problem.

First thing to do is look at the current layout of the area of the project. Using my example of the bathroom, go and look at where the existing toilet/shower/sink(s) and so on are located. If you're doing your kitchen, do the same thing.

My main piece of advice is to leave the new fixtures (sinks, toilet, etc.) in the same/similar location. The best thing to do is to plan around the location(s) where all existing supply lines, waste, vents, and so forth are installed. That is, put the new shower, toilet, and so on right where the old ones are now.

When dealing with plumbing, distance equals money, so moving plumbing services a long way will blow most budgets out of the water. Stay "local" to where all existing items are located.

Next thing to do is to get a blank piece of paper and hand draw what you'd like the layout to look like. Do at least two of them: one as though you are looking at it from the ceiling (plan view) and one from standing in front of the wall (elevation view). I would focus on the elevation view for the vanity wall. You may want to do one for each of the walls, but don't make it too complicated for yourself. It doesn't have to be pretty, but it will make you think about where things go.

Other items to consider:

- Where do you want the vanity? How are you buying this? Premade or custom built?
- One or two sinks?
- Any medicine cabinet(s)? Recessed or surface mounted?
- New mirror(s)?
- Towel rack(s)? How many? Where? What style?
- Power outlets? How many? Where?

This is where your previous research will start to pay dividends as you already have an idea of what you want, and we're now moving into the where-are-we-going-to-put-it phase.

The scope statement is taking shape without you even knowing it and before you've started any writing. By doing this work up front, you can see the type of things that are going to help you write it and why it's important to do it.

At this stage, you're now in a good position to start typing this out (you can handwrite it, too, if that's your preference).

Follow the same categories as I've shown you in the example. If you're not using any of them, delete them. If you're doing something else, add it in. No problem.

You should now start to see that there are quite a few more layers to this than meets the eye, and that is why things end up being more expensive than it first seems.

The tricky part of this is being able to peel apart what you want each subtrade to do and articulating it accordingly. The example will guide you through the types of things you need to write and this should help make it easier.

You don't have to have all the finishes finalized before starting the scope statement. You can continue to toss around ideas of different sizes and styles. The infrastructure work (water supply, drains, etc.) will have to be done irrespective of the end result.

A piece of advice to pass on: I have always stayed away from telling the builders and subtrades *how* I want something done. Instead, I've focused on telling them *what* I want done. It has kept me in good standing with them. They are the experts. Let them do what they know best.

An important item to remember when doing the scope statement is finding out in advance if you will need a permit from your local jurisdiction to perform this type of work in your home.

I'm not going to provide direction either way on this. You will have to get this information yourself as well as the costs involved. Be very mindful that obtaining a permit may trigger other requirements that are unrelated to the job itself (e.g., upgrade sewer lateral, etc.). Go in with your eyes wide open.

If you need a permit, you'll need drawings. I've inserted language you can use to engage an architect in the scope example to help you out. If it's not needed, then delete it.

CHAPTER FOUR

FINANCIALS: THE ESTIMATE

The best way to understand the budget and what your project might cost is to prepare an estimate for yourself. Otherwise, you have no visibility of the approximate cost of the project before you begin on this journey.

An unfortunate reality of any home upgrade (or commercial one, for that matter) is the ability—or inability—to fund the work. You might have a budget of, say, $20,000 to do the bathroom at home, but the cost of what you want done is $40,000. That's a big problem.

You might think it's easy to call up a builder, get them to come around, look at a job, and prepare an estimate. It could be. But they'll guess at a lot of things, including what they think you need, and most likely, they'll work it all out on scrap paper. That doesn't help anyone whatsoever. Most importantly, they'll figure out pretty quickly if you're a time waster or genuine. Then they'll react accordingly.

If you want to get a builder to look at your job, then please be respectful of their time. Respect your own time, too. Remember that their efforts (and accuracy) will match yours. So my strong advice is to put the effort in up front. They will reciprocate this with you, and you'll get better results. Otherwise, your project could end up costing you more time and money.

Doing your own estimate initially is going to be daunting. But it doesn't need to be that way, and I'm going to help you through it.

The estimate is best done after you've compiled the scope statement. So do the scope first. That way, you're able to objectively look at the job with all its bits and pieces and put some form of task hours and materials behind it all.

I've provided an example at the end of the book to help you out with this. If you're doing a bathroom, it's virtually all there for you. However, if it's something else (kitchen?), replace the trades I've got there with the relevant ones.

Let's look at an example of how you would try and work something out.

We'll focus on the tiling for a bathroom and assume that the footprint of the bathroom isn't changing from what it is now.

The type of tasks to complete the tiling are as follows (note: this list is not exhaustive):

- Prepare the substrate for the new floor material, including the mortar bed for the shower.
- Lay the tile on the floors/walls/shower/bath.
- Install the grout.

If I were to estimate this, here's how I would do it. I would consider how long I thought it might take a skilled tradesman to do all this work. Looking at the descriptions in the previous paragraph, I would estimate that to do all this in a typical bathroom will probably take something like eight man-days or sixty-four hours (eight days times eight hours).

It doesn't matter if the tiler has a helper (they most likely will) and the work is done in four calendar days. It is still going to require sixty-four hours to complete this work.

Once I have that, the next thing to do is find the local labor rate for tilers, add the cost of the material, and now you've got the approximate pricing for the tile work.

You're probably wondering, "How do I find the labor rate?"

It will require a little legwork, but the first place to start is our old friend Google. If that doesn't give you what you need, call the local union shop (if there is one). Tell them what you're doing and why you're seeking information. They should help you. Also, try the friends and family network. There's bound to be someone who knows someone and so forth who can give you the data.

Materials are a little easier to source and price. You can visit your local hardware store, or you can access stores online and look at the products and prices they provide. Failing that, larger chains like Home Depot or Lowes have local stores and websites with lots of information to help you figure out what the materials cost. If you want specialized materials, you will most likely have to cast your net a lot wider to find them. Once again, Google will get you on your way.

For the larger areas of work, such as tiling or drywall, you will need to do a quick measure to find out the square footage/meters. It doesn't have to be absolutely accurate, but get a tape measure and figure out the length and width to give you the dimensions. Suppliers will typically work out their costs on this basis when calculating their prices.

It's also okay to allocate an allowance for materials if you're not sure (I do this regularly in commercial jobs). For example, if you're doing your bathroom and don't know how much plywood or wood/metal studs might be required for floors/walls/ceilings, put in, say, $1,000 for it as a place-holder. It doesn't matter if it's not completely accurate. It might cost more but probably not a lot more for a bathroom, or it may even cost less. The critical thing is to include *a dollar amount.*

Continuing with the bathroom example, the plumber will need all sorts of miscellaneous supplies—pipe, fasteners, washers, and so on. The same is applicable to an electrician—electrical wiring (Romex, etc.), junction boxes, outlet trim, and so forth. Once again, you don't need to know the exact cost of these items, but be sure to include some material pricing in your own budget. These items *will* be required, and you will be charged for them.

If it makes you feel any better, I've learned that estimating is more art than science, so it's not a matter of being 100 percent accurate. It's about knowing it has to be included and then providing a dollar amount for the work. Remember, we're trying to reduce the amount of surprises that occur in the project.

Make sure you add in your own contingency depending on your level of comfort with your research and most definitely consider the age of the house. Older houses will almost certainly need more infrastructure upgrades than you think, and maybe even asbestos removal, so make sure this is factored into your estimation and thinking.

I'm confident that once you've completed a scope statement and have done the research on the labor and materials, you're going to get somewhere close to your estimated costs.

Don't worry if you get this wrong. It's not a test about being correct or incorrect. It's about reversing your thinking to put yourself in the shoes of the builder to work out the real cost of a project and then to compare it to the affordability within your own budget.

The builder will look at a job and put together an estimate similar to the one I've shown you. If they get it wrong, it costs them money.

Remember that the labor time to do something is the key point to your overall budget. You won't be able to change that. Labor is your biggest cost, so by getting a better understanding of how long something takes, it will make your life and the costs of your project more palatable and real than if you hadn't done the work ahead of time.

Once you've got an idea of the approximate cost versus your own budget, you may need to realign your thinking to reach a realistic decision. It's much better to make these decisions now rather than trying to make changes halfway through construction with a big hole in your bathroom floor!

CHOOSING A BUILDER OR GENERAL CONTRACTOR

Now that you've done the scope statement, had a crack at the estimate, and discovered that you think you can afford something close to it, what's next?

You need to find a builder or general contractor (GC). They are a key part of your project.

The construction industry has many parts to it and many people who derive their living from it. Most builders and subtrades are just like you and me. They want to make a

CHOOSING A BUILDER OR GENERAL CONTRACTOR · 35

comfortable living and charge you a fair and reasonable rate for their services.

You will certainly come across some questionable people, no doubt about that. But like every other significant purchase you make in your life (house, car, etc.), you will need to do your research to reduce the likelihood of that happening.

Be prepared to ask questions of the prospective builder. Compile a discussion list of the items that are important to you. Talk to others who have used them and find out their business practices and ethics. If it helps, use a referral engine (Yelp, Angie's List, etc.).

I'd suggest that you settle on one to two builders that you like and then decide how you want to proceed.

There are a multitude of ways to go about this, but I'll simplify it down to two of the easier options:

1. Choose one builder from the ones you've spoken to and negotiate the job.
2. Solicit bids (tenders) from multiple builders (hard bid).

Either method is okay, but there are a few pertinent facts to consider.

NEGOTIATED

- This is a methodology whereby the builder will tell you what it will cost them to run the job, otherwise known as general conditions or prelims (supervision, project management, etc.). You will also agree upon the fees for the job. This can be shown as overhead and markup.
- You need to be comfortable with this once it's finalized, as there is no going back on the agreement after it's confirmed.
- If you're concerned about the stated fees, do more research in your local area and find out the going rate for each job task.
- Ask yourself, "What would you want to get paid if this were your business?"
- If you're still stuck, use 10 percent to 12 percent as a starting point. It's fair and it's reasonable for both parties.
- Remember, they want to make a profit on your job and they're entitled to it, just as much as you are entitled to receive a decent product from the money you've paid.
- Here is how the mechanics of this works:
  ○ Once the rates have been agreed to, the builder shows you the actual cost for each of the respective sections of work, applies their fees, and then the pricing for this section of work is completed.
  ○ You can ask for multiple prices from any of the sub-trades, but remember that each ask will add time and a bit of cost to the general conditions. It is recommended that you do this as once you've seen multiple subtrade

quotes, you can assist in the selection and know the price you're paying and what you're getting for it.

   ○ An advantage to using this methodology is that the builder should be passing on any savings they find. For example, if they priced installing new studs in the wall but discover that the original studs are in good condition and do not need to be replaced, then the labor and material cost of this and all associated work should be credited back.

- This can be quite beneficial to the customer, but make sure that you understand there is no known ceiling on the pricing until everything in the scope is finalized and the subtrades are engaged and under contract.

HARD BID/TENDER

- The builder will give you a lump sum price to do the job. You can ask for it to be broken out by trade. I would.
- This pricing will include their risk—that is, items that they're not sure about. However, a scope statement should also reduce your own exposure to the unknowns. It's a win for both of you.
- The builder is not expected to share any savings they find along the way.
- The biggest advantage with this methodology is that you obtain certainty in your pricing—the price you see is the price you pay (subject to change orders and variations that you ask for).

One word of advice: Don't think you can be the builder yourself. You can't. It's as simple as that. In some jurisdictions, it's illegal. Even if it is legal, there are many issues that could arise that could be disastrous. Safety, insurance, labor/material orders, sequencing, and coordination are just a few items that a rookie wouldn't know are required.

It's simple. Don't do it.

Get your mind around paying someone who knows what is required, can do the work safely, has the relevant insurances, and so forth and can successfully source the appropriate labor and materials. That is, the builder or GC.

I've come across many weekend warriors in the commercial arena, and these people, although well-meaning, cause more delays and cost than you can imagine.

Stick to what you know best (whatever career that may be) and leave the construction to those who have the experience.

WHICH ONE?

Once you've decided on the methodology, it will require more work from you to find your construction partner. Let's assume you've chosen a local builder. Now it's time to pick up the phone and call them.

Depending on the size of the company, it's best to speak to the owner, if possible. Why the owner? They depend on people like you for their business to survive and flourish. You can be assured they will be quite receptive to discussing your job with them.

Tell them the overall objective. For example, "My house is seventy years old with an original bathroom, and it's time to upgrade it. I've put together a scope statement and would now like to get things going."

Ask them what they would like to do next. Most likely, they will want to come and meet you and look at the premises. Find out if they will provide an estimate based on the scope statement and site conditions. Everyone will do it differently, so be prepared to be flexible when working with them, but make sure your own needs are met.

Whatever is decided, send them the scope statement beforehand so they can start to think about the job.

Now, don't be alarmed if when they are looking at the on-site conditions, they pick up things you've missed. That's perfectly fine. Remember, they are the experts. But if you've spent the time doing the scope well, I'm confident they won't come up with many items you've missed.

COMPARE PRICING

Once you've decided on the methodology as described in the previous section and you've chosen your partner for the project, I'm going to suggest that you sit down with them and compare their pricing with yours.

Why do this now?

It is the final step before signing a contract, and this is where you are going to find out how far (if at all) your budget differs from theirs. There is absolutely nothing wrong with doing this. In fact, you *need* to do it.

At this stage, by doing the scope and your own budget, you've significantly reduced the gap in expectations of what you think it would cost versus the builder's view had you not done it in the first place.

I'm going to (almost) guarantee, you have just saved yourself a significant amount of pain. How?

If your numbers are close to theirs, fantastic. Job well done. If not, you can come clean with your estimate and ask them for theirs. You will find out now what you've missed (if anything) and that's perfectly okay—that's the educational part of this and a great way to learn.

If your budget is blown, all is not lost. You have a chance to do something about it now.

Here is the time to discuss value engineering options if your estimates are over budget. Value engineering is when you look for options for material/method substitutions in order to reduce costs without sacrificing the end result and functionality. The builder should help you with this.

This is why, yet again, I'm going to reiterate, you need to do some preparatory work beforehand. The more the better. There is no getting around it. I am repeating myself—no apologies for doing that!

The final item to look at is the all-important exclusions/clarifications. The exclusions can be a budget and project killer, but here is where your scope statement will repay you in spades. If it's written in the scope, it's up to the builder or GC to tell you they're not doing it. Otherwise, it's included. If it's in, great. If not, ask why.

CONTRACTS

This is a necessary evil that people doing work of any substance will need to cover. So if it's for a full bathroom or kitchen remodel, you will definitely need a contract. Painting the lounge room? No contract needed.

If you don't create your own contract, then you'll be stuck with the terms and conditions of the builder. This is not something I'd advise unless you've read the builder's specifications along with the prices and they are acceptable to you.

I'm not going to suggest a specific contract you should or shouldn't use. You will find many contracts in the marketplace, and this in itself, is a whole book on its own. There are standards produced in each jurisdiction, and if you were to use one of those, you should be fine. I'd suggest to Google something along the lines of "contract for residential construction," and the results of your search will give you a place to start.

Builders are used to seeing standard contracts, and they know their contents. Just make sure the contract you're signing is fair and reasonable and it protects both parties.

The rule of thumb with a construction contract is that once it's signed, it's sent to the top drawer of the filing cabinet, never to see the light of day again. If you must review it, then it means something's gone wrong. My advice is to discuss any disagreement you might have, resolve it amicably, and stay away from engaging the legal profession.

CHAPTER SIX

CONSTRUCTION

This is where the rubber meets the road. In my experience, when writing scope statements and budgets before work has commenced, approximately 80 percent of the work for you is done. Now it's the builder's turn.

Some items I'm going to suggest are things you need to manage to keep the building process moving along at a reasonable pace.

CASH FLOW

You should never start any work of a substantial nature without having the funds available for use. That means you should not start any building project unless you have money in a cash account as well as funds available through a credit card.

When you are presented with an invoice for the work completed, my advice would be to make sure each item, purchase, and task has been detailed in line items so you can see the percentage completed for each work task. Don't accept a lump sum payment request.

If the invoice seems fair and reasonable, don't quibble. Pay it quickly. Tradespeople and suppliers will be more responsive about all sorts of things if you pay them in a timely manner. A lot of them will reciprocate by doing more for you without charging the extras.

One thing I'm going to strongly recommend: Do *not* hang on to the invoice and play games with the supplier by stringing out the payments. That is wrong. If they've done the work, you're happy with it, and it's commensurate with the progress on site, pay them. It's only fair.

If you have any concerns with an invoice, pick up the phone, make an appointment with the builder or supplier, and then go see them. By this stage, you've discovered their bona fides, and if there is something you're not happy with, you should be able to get a swift resolution.

Remember, if you've done your homework, you're more than likely dealing with someone like you who is hardworking, honest, fair, and reasonable and they are just trying to eke out a living and take care of their families.

Show them the respect they deserve. You will get repaid in all sorts of ways.

SCHEDULE

Although the renovation of a bathroom or kitchen is a major imposition to you, bear in mind that the builder and sub-trades all have other jobs for other people like you, at various stages of completion. And they are juggling other priorities for other customers as well as yours.

Builders and subtrades have staff members who get sick, go AWOL, must look after sick children, and so on. Just like you. If you're able to keep this in the back of your mind throughout the project, it will make the stress levels more tolerable for you if things are delayed.

Compiling a scope statement and budget estimate should give you a sense of how long this project should take. Have a look at the number of hours you've inserted in the estimate and you won't be too far away. Don't stress if you miss some things and it goes longer.

Add in two to three weeks to the start and end of your time-line and that should give you a good starting point for how long it should take. Be sure to factor in other items that you want that have long lead times.

Once you've selected your builder and agreed on the scope and the price, have them produce a schedule. It will allow you to monitor the progress.

One thing I am going to stress about the schedule: The builder will most likely at some stage end up doing things out of the sequence that is shown. This is not something you should worry about. It happens regularly. In fact, I can't recall a commercial project that I've worked on where this hasn't happened.

It's normal and it's fine. A construction project is a living thing that changes frequently.

The critical item to understand relating to the schedule is communication—a dialogue between the two parties that needs to be open and honest.

If things are delayed, listen to what the builder is telling you. Ask questions, but if you're prepared properly, slight schedule overruns shouldn't be a project killer for you.

CHAPTER SEVEN

CHANGE ORDERS AND VARIATIONS

This is the bane of every client's existence, but change orders and variations are an important facet of the construction process. If you don't embrace them properly, they will simply run you over.

No matter how much preparatory work you've undertaken for a project, there will be the inevitable item(s) that come up that no one foresaw.

For example, once the walls have been removed, it may be obvious that there is dry rot (for wood) or rust (for metal) everywhere and the studs have to be replaced. Neither you nor the builder could have known that before starting the project, and there will be costs for doing this work.

Similarly, if you (the client) change your mind about an item in the project, and you are absolutely entitled to do this, just remember there is a cost (usually) for changing your mind.

The goal of this is to keep these to a minimum and within your budget. If you've done the work via a scope statement, these monetary costs should be small. But, and here it is again, do the work at the start and this will not be as painful as if you had done nothing.

If there is something unexpected that comes up, spend the time to look at it and understand what it is and why the additional work must be undertaken. Talk it over with your builder. If you've chosen correctly, they should be more than happy to explain to you what's happened and why.

Don't be afraid to ask for a breakdown of the pricing. This will give you an itemized view of the new costs and what's driving anything unnecessary or larger than expected.

Make sure you've agreed before the job has begun what the markup on this additional work will be. That will save some possible aggravation when you are presented with the bill.

The suggested contingency shown on the estimate is exactly what should be used for these situations.

CHAPTER EIGHT

EXPECTATIONS

A significant reason I'm writing this book is that I believe one of the biggest challenges in construction projects (this applies equally with commercial as well as residential) is that clients' eyes are typically bigger than their wallets.

I fully realize that everyone wants a Mercedes-Benz for the price of a Datsun Sunny, but unfortunately, it just doesn't work that way. We need to reset those expectations.

The biggest factor I've found is the understanding (or unfortunately, the lack thereof) of what it actually takes to do something.

This is not insurmountable, but it is a critical part of any construction project. The simple saying that time is money is an apt description.

For example, how long do you think it would take to demolish a bathroom down to the studs? Some people think it could be done in a day. No chance. Try two to three days with two people. And don't forget the cost of the dumpster.

So why do I bring up expectations? The reason is that when you prepare both a scope statement and an estimate or budget, they will more likely give you a better understanding of what it *really* takes to do a job. We are undertaking some reverse engineering in the thought process.

The reality is that the vast majority of projects begin with an idea or a need to do something, along with the abstract thinking of the costs associated with it, without much thought put into how it's going to get completed.

Having you write a scope statement is an attempt to get you to alter your thinking in order to change the result. Remember that the definition of insanity is to do something the same way but expecting a different outcome.

Writing your own scope statement and budget estimate is going to help you think about it from the builder's perspective, and it will make you decide what you want.

I can't guarantee that it will necessarily stop the questionable practices that occur from time to time in the industry, but I'm confident it will limit them.

CONCLUSION

The scope and budget examples given are from someone (me) who's used to doing this on a daily basis. Don't beat yourself up if things take you longer than I've indicated. The important point of this book is to get people prepared in the right way, up front, before any work has commenced.

I've also laid out the steps involved to get you to this point. It's not exhaustive nor is it the holy grail, but it will get you on your way and help alleviate some of the stress.

It will also assist your overall mental state, help you gain respect from the construction people involved, and you will learn a lot along the way. I'm certain it will be much more fun doing your project this way than doing it on the run or relying on someone else to do it for you. With a budget and a scope statement, you won't have to wonder why things turned out so different from your original expectations. People are not mind readers.

And yes, people in the construction industry make mistakes, just like you. So once something has been identified and a resolution has been reached, leave them alone to fix it.

I've deliberately kept the verbiage in the book as a whole to a minimum. I could go into far more detail in each of the chapters, but I think that defeats the purpose.

The key for success is to get you to alter your thought process and use the tools provided (scope statement and estimate). These are your big takeaway ticket items.

I want to point out that this book is not written with the intent of providing all solutions to all scenarios for all people. But I'm hoping that your project has at least been a little more fun than it otherwise may have been.

APPENDIX 1

PROJECT SCOPE STATEMENT

PROJECT NAME: BATHROOM RENOVATION

PREPARED BY: DAMIAN CARROLL

DATE: OCTOBER 15, 2018

PROJECT DESCRIPTION:	• The existing bathroom is old and appears to be original to the house when it was built in 1937.
	• The tile work is starting to crack and come away from the wall. The grout has clearly passed its use-by date.
	• The bathtub is in good condition and could be reused if it will fit into the new layout.
	• The client will be supplying some materials. These will be listed in detail via each deliverable.
	• A summary of the changes include:
	  ◦ Toilet to remain in the same location
	  ◦ New bathtub in the location of the corner of the existing vanity
	  ◦ Laundry chute to be removed
	  ◦ Shower to be relocated to the area of the laundry chute
	  ◦ New vanity unit in the location of the existing shower and bathtub
	  ◦ New tile flooring
	  ◦ New lighting
	  ◦ New medicine cabinets
	  ◦ New heated towel rack
	  ◦ Existing HVAC outlet is redundant and is to be covered over

PROJECT NAME: BATHROOM RENOVATION

PROJECT DELIVERABLES:	The following is a summary of subproducts whose full and satisfactory delivery is required to complete the project successfully:

1. Architectural services
2. General conditions and preliminaries
3. Demolition
4. Rough carpentry
5. Millwork and joinery (cabinets)
6. Roofing
7. Doors
8. Glazing
9. Drywall
10. Ceramic tile
11. Floor covering
12. Painting
13. Glazing
14. Ceramic tile
15. Plumbing
16. Electrical
17. Other building works
18. Client-supplied materials

The successful company (or companies) will be required to undertake the following work:

DELIVERABLE #1	Architectural Services

- Review of the client's design and brief requirements in conjunction with this work statement.
- Ensure a complete measure of the affected areas is undertaken.
- Preliminary assessment of regulatory and other requirements.
- Develop the design including plans, elevations, sections, and other details or schedules sufficient to fully explain the design.
- Engage, coordinate, and integrate the design work of all service consultants (if required).
- Prepare schedule of materials and finishes.
- Prepare schedules and other documents required for tendering in PDF format.
- Prepare schedules and other documents required for construction in PDF format.
- Respond to requests for information or clarification as required.
- Provide supplementary details and information as required.
- Provide technical assistance as required during the construction process.
- Respond to queries during construction as required by the client.
- Interpret and clarify ambiguities in documents.
- Ensure all documents are prepared in order to obtain planning approval and pay associated fees to the relevant jurisdiction for the work permit.

PROJECT NAME: BATHROOM RENOVATION

DELIVERABLE #2	General Conditions and Preliminaries

- Project management.
- Supervision. Includes truck costs, safety and first-aid supplies, communications (email, phone, etc.).

DELIVERABLE #3	Demolition

- Remove and appropriately dispose of the following items:
  - Existing floor tile
  - Existing toilet
  - Existing vanity
  - Existing wall tile
  - Existing mortar bed under the shower
  - Existing laundry chute
  - Existing drywall and hard lid ceiling
  - Existing lighting
  - Existing bathtub
  - Existing subfloor
  - Existing window
  - Existing supply/waste/vent lines and electrical wiring that cannot be reused
- All plumbing fixtures are to be made safe by the plumber.
- All electrical fixtures are to be made safe by the electrician.
- Existing door and frame are to remain and be reused.

Note: All existing wood framing and floor joists are to remain if in good condition.

DELIVERABLE #4	Rough Carpentry

- Provide labor and materials for the following items:
  - Install new subfloor over existing floor joists. Includes the appropriate fill for the removed laundry chute.
  - Construct one pony wall approximately 2' AFL at the western end of the bathtub location.
  - Construct curb to enclose the shower in the location of the demolished laundry chute.
  - Prepare the existing wall joists for the installation of two new recessed medicine cabinets.
  - Prepare the existing wall joists for the installation of a new inset in the shower. This is to be approximately 5' AFL and centered on the appropriate wall as close as possible.
  - Prepare the existing wall joists for the installation of a new heated towel rail.
  - Prepare the existing ceiling joists for the installation of a new exhaust fan inside the shower.
  - Install one new window where the old window was removed. Dimensions are to match the existing opening.
  - Install one access panel in the wall on the stairwell for the new bath.
  - Fill in the existing hole that was previously used as a laundry chute.
  - Install one new vanity unit in the location shown on the sketch. This will be delivered to the client's site downstairs.
  - Install framing around the existing vent line running in the wall behind the toilet. This line will not be relocated.
  - Install new plywood subfloor over the floor joists once all rough-ins have been completed.
  - Install new waterproofing membrane on the new subfloor and shower areas.
  - Install towel rings, towel rails, and robe hooks in the locations shown by the client. Materials to be supplied by the client.

DELIVERABLE #5	Millwork/Joinery (Cabinets)

- Provide labor and materials for the following items:
  - Install in place the vanity supplied by the client. This will need to be moved from the living room downstairs.
  - Provide any cutouts necessary so that the plumbing fixtures and fittings can be installed.

DELIVERABLE #6	Roofing

- There are no alterations required to the roof.

DELIVERABLE #7	Doors

- There is no alteration to the existing door. It is to be reused.

DELIVERABLE #8   Glazing

- Supply and install the following items:
  - Two new 1/2" tempered glass fixed panels. These are to be finished at approximately 7" AFL and are to incorporate the pony wall at the end of the bathtub.
  - Include the appropriate U-Channels.
  - One new 3/8" tempered glass door to match the height of the adjacent panels.
  - Hardware: CB Laurence brushed nickel hinges, door pulls, clamps, and U-Channel.

DELIVERABLE #9   Drywall

- Provide labor and materials for the following items:
  - Install new drywall throughout the entire bathroom. Includes hard lid ceiling.
  - Ensure the shower area is installed with the appropriate green board.
  - All new drywall is to be taped with a level 4 finish, ready for finish application.

DELIVERABLE #10   Ceramic Tile

- Supply and install the following items:
  - Rittenhouse 3" x 6" arctic white subway tile on all walls (except shower) up to 5' AFL
  - Rittenhouse Shelf Rail (2" x 6") on all walls (except shower) above subway tile
  - Liners Deco Arctic White (1/2" x 6") for shower inset
  - Lantern mosaic tile LA-3 glossy white for shower inset
  - Semigloss field tile (4¼" x 4¼") white tile for the shower curb
  - Cannes tile for base excluding shower (4½" x 6")
  - Hexagon floor tile (3") homed in excluding shower
  - Hexagon floor tile (1") homed in shower only
  - Quarter-round arctic white tile for the shower base and pony wall
  - Grout: 1/8" line, Delorean Gray (#165)
  - Flooring to be thin-set base excluding shower and bathtub
  - Mortar bed for the shower base only, inside curb

DELIVERABLE #11   Floor Covering

- As the floor will be tile, there is no additional floor covering required.

DELIVERABLE #12   Painting

- Provide labor and materials for the following items:
  - Paint all drywall that does not have any other finish applied (tile, etc.).
  - Color TBD.

PROJECT NAME: BATHROOM RENOVATION

| **DELIVERABLE #13** | Hydraulics Services (Plumbing) |

- Provide labor and materials for the following items:
  - Make safe all items scheduled for demolition.
  - Install all new supply, waste, and vent lines per the revised layout.
  - Rough in all fixtures per the provided sketch.
  - Connect all trim upon completion of the work, prior to use.
- **Note:** The toilet is to remain in the same location.
- Plumber to procure all fixtures. Client to pay warehouse directly.
  - One (1) Kohler K-715-0 bathtub
  - Two (2) Kohler Archer K-11076-4-CP faucets for the vanity
  - One (1) Kohler Archer K-T45849-4-CP tub filler for the bath
  - One (1) Kohler Archer K-3551-0 toilet
  - One (1) Kohler Archer K-11054-CP toilet roll holder
  - One (1) Kohler Archer K-T11078-4-CP shower fixture
  - Two (2) Kohler Archer K-11051-CP towel bars
  - Three (3) Kohler Archer K-11057-CP towel rings
  - Two (2) Kohler Archer K-11055-CP door hooks

| **DELIVERABLE #14** | HVAC/Mechanical Services (Air-Conditioning) |

- The existing HVAC outlet is redundant. No changes to it are required. It is to be covered over with the new wall.

| **DELIVERABLE #15** | Electrical Services |

- Provide labor and materials for the following items:
  - Make safe all items scheduled for demolition.
  - Remove all existing "knob and tube" wiring currently in use.
  - Install three (3) new light fixtures on the wall above the vanity.
  - Install one (1) new steam-resistant light inside the shower.
  - Install one (1) new light fixture in the same location where the original light was removed.
  - All light fixtures supplied by the client to the site.
  - Install three (3) new double power outlets in the location shown on the sketch. The height AFL will be at different levels as required.
  - Install one (1) new three-gang switch to replace the existing switch. One (1) each for the exhaust fan, lights above the vanity, and light in the shower/open area.
  - Prepare all new conduit and wiring for the lighting and services that meets the current code.

| **DELIVERABLE #16** | Other Building Works |

- Ensure that appropriate floor protection is in place throughout the affected areas for the duration of the work.

PROJECT NAME: BATHROOM RENOVATION

DELIVERABLE #17	Client-Supplied Material

- One (1) 20 yd³ (up to 2 tons) dumpster for the demolition spoil. This will be available for two (2) weeks only once it is delivered to the site.
- Two (2) recessed medicine cabinets
- One (1) vanity unit (already assembled)
- One (1) heated towel rack
- One (1) light fixture for the center of the room
- Three (3) can lights for above the medicine cabinets
- One (1) downlight for inside the shower
- One (1) exhaust fan for inside the shower
- The existing door is to be reused.

Note: Assume that all materials will be supplied to the site by the client unless otherwise specified.

The client has an approved budget allocation for this project. This figure is deemed to include all costs associated with meeting the deliverables listed.

PROJECT OBJECTIVES: In order for this project to be considered successful for the client, the following project objectives must be met:

1. Scope Objectives
2. Time Objectives
3. Cost Objectives
4. Quality Objectives

SCHEDULE OBJECTIVES Work is to commence as soon as approval has been given by the client. The subcontractors performing the work will be expected to adhere to the agreed timeline for the works. Progress payment will be provided for the respective subtrades on a fortnightly basis and in line with the progress made on the site.

QUALITY MEASURES All contractors are required to operate a recognized and approved audited system of quality control, which should be monitored and measured over the life cycle of the project.

KNOWN EXCLUSIONS The following works are specifically excluded from this contract:

- Certification or guarantees confirming that all existing work and/or services are to the required standard or regulatory requirements.
- Any remaining furniture items are to be left in place and all works carried on around these objects.

Once this scope statement has been signed off by the client per below, this approves the procurement of the appropriate materials to commence on site.

Damian Carroll

_____

Signature

_____

Date

APPENDIX 2

PROJECT ESTIMATE

DELIVERABLE		TYPE	UNITS	RATE	COST
1	Architectural Services		1	$3,000	$3,000
2	GCs/Prelims				$7,500
		Project Management	1	$2,500	
		Supervision	1	$5,000	
3	Demolition		32	$50	$1,600
4	Rough Carpentry				$4.550
	Subfloor	Labor	24	$50	
	Subfloor	Materials	1	$300	
	Stud/Frame Preparation	Labor	32	$50	
	Stud/Frame Preparation	Materials	1	$400	
	Waterproofing Membrane	Labor	2	$50	
	Waterproofing Membrane	Materials	1	$250	
	Miscellaneous	Labor	8	$50	
	Miscellaneous	Materials	1	$300	

DELIVERABLE		TYPE	UNITS	RATE	COST
5	Millwork/ Joinery (Cabinets)				$100
		Labor	2	$50	
		Materials	0	$—	
6	Roofing				$—
		Labor	0	$—	
		Materials	0	$—	
7	Doors				$—
		Labor	0	$—	
		Materials	0	$—	
8	Glazing				$1,500
		Labor	12	$75	
		Materials	1	$600	
9	Drywall				$2,800
	Sheetrock	Labor	32	$50	
	Sheetrock	Materials	1	$500	
	Taping	Lot	1	$700	
10	Ceramic Tile				$6,700
		Labor	64	$50	
		Materials	1	$3,500	
11	Floor Covering				$—
		Labor	0	$—	
		Materials	0	$—	
12	Painting				$1,040
		Labor	16	$40	
		Materials	1	$400	

DELIVERABLE		TYPE	UNITS	RATE	COST
13	Hydraulics (Plumbing)				$10,500
		Labor	40	$75	
		Materials	1	$7,500	
14	HVAC/ Mech (Air-Conditioning)				$—
		Labor	0	$—	
		Materials	0	$—	
15	Electrical				$2,300
		Labor	24	$75	
		Materials	1	$500	
16	Other Building Works				$750
		Protection	1	$250	
		Other (Misc.)	1	$500	
		Other	0	$—	
17	Client-Supplied Items				$3,400
		Dumpster	1	$500	
		Medicine Cabinets	2	$300	
		Vanity Unit	1	$1,500	
		Heated Towel Rack	1	$150	
		Lighting	1	$500	
		Exhaust Fan	1	$150	
SUBTOTAL					$45,740

DELIVERABLE	TYPE	UNITS	RATE	COST
GC/ BUILDER'S MARKUP			10%	$4,574
ESTIMATE TOTAL				**$50,314**
CONTINGENCY*			15%	$7,547
BUDGET TOTAL				$57,861

*The older the building, the more this should be.

Notes:

- Assume eight-hour days.
- Apply local labor and material rates.

ACKNOWLEDGMENTS

I have to start by thanking my awesome wife, Elissa. From helping me make sense with the early drafts to being a sounding board on the cover and then assisting with keeping the kids occupied to get the writing completed. The overall support has been outstanding, and she was a critical part to this book getting completed. Thanks, dear.

My parents, Terry and Ann, have always provided wonderful support and guidance throughout my life and I wouldn't be the person I am today if it wasn't for them. They have had their hands full dealing with our disabled brother for decades, but they have been there for me and my other siblings time and again without fail.

The inspiration for this book and the want to help people who need it in the construction industry come from my mentor in the game, Steve Broadbent. He showed extraordinary patience throughout the training until I started to get it. Most importantly, he instilled the confidence in me that I can hold my own anywhere under any conditions. It enabled me to pack up and move halfway around the world on a whim. I couldn't have achieved the professional results I have without his guidance and help. Cancer got him before this was finished, but his teachings and wisdom live on through this book and anytime I have the opportunity to assist others.

The Scribe team have been extraordinarily patient with me while we've had to juggle children, the blasted virus, as well as battling a temporary move to Australia. Without the support from my Publishing Manager, Maggie (the poor soul who had to deal with me), and the rest of the amazing people involved at Scribe, none of this would have been a reality.

ABOUT THE AUTHOR

DAMIAN CARROLL has worked in the construction industry for over fifteen years and written hundreds of scopes. After seeing how often a good scope statement can save your skin and how badly things can go without one, he wrote this book to help inexperienced homeowners create the home of their dreams at a fair and reasonable price. To learn more and connect with Damian, please visit www.damiancarroll.com or www.thescopestatement.com.

CPSIA information can be obtained
at www.ICGtesting.com
Printed in the USA
FSHW011020170821